A DEPENDABLE SIBLING

- BE DEFERENTIAL
- LOVE AND CARE
- SIBLINGS
- STRONG BOND

ALEX RICHARD

TABLE OF CONTENTS

INTRODUCTION 3
CHAPTER ONE 4
SETTING A GENUINE MODEL 4
FOSTERING A DECENT RELATIONSHIP 10
EXCEEDING ALL EXPECTATIONS 18
CHAPTER TWO 23
WAYS OF DRAWING NEAR TO YOUR SIBLING 23
CHAPTER THREE 38
CHARACTERISTICS OF A DECENT SIBLING 38
HOW MIGHT I IMPROVE AS A SIBLING? 50
CHAPTER FOUR 54
CONCLUSION 54

INTRODUCTION

Being an older kin is a gift and an obligation. Kin competition is normal, however more youthful kin can likewise be your partners, team promoters or dearest companions. Whether you have a stressed relationship with your more youthful kin or you simply need to turn out to be nearer to them, there are open doors for you to be a superior elder sibling. The interaction will require some work, however a superior relationship with your kin is a beneficial prize.

CHAPTER ONE

SETTING A GENUINE MODEL

➢ **BE DEFERENTIAL**

It means a lot to set a model for your kin by continuously being conscious. Be deferential to them, obviously, however you ought to likewise be conscious to your folks, your instructors, your companions, and, surprisingly, wonderful outsiders! Being deferential will help them a ton throughout everyday life and in the event that they gain it from somebody they truly regard, it will end up being a long lasting habit.

- **TRY NOT TO DISRESPECT YOUR FOLKS OR EDUCATORS**

Amenably contend assuming issues come up yet in any case do everything you're said and show your kin how it's finished.

- **BE CAPABLE**

Your kin to figure out how actually should be capable. Try not to take medications or liquor and do stay aware of your errands and help around the house. Accomplish something useful in school yet be modest about your grades. Find a new line of work on the off chance that your timetable permits and set aside your cash dependably. This helps you yet it likewise sets an extraordinary model for them. They'll see that difficult work and penance pay off.

➢ UTILIZE GREAT LANGUAGE

Most certainly don't show them each terrible word in the book, yet utilizing great language likewise implies talking great. Talk accurately and with the best language structure and jargon you can make due. They'll get on your language and glean some significant experience. Great discourse is much of the time an indication of superior instruction and numerous businesses think of it as fundamental, so you'll set them up for a long period of progress.

➢ STAY AWAY FROM BRUTALITY

You ought to make an effort not to be fierce towards your kin and set an additional genuine model by not being savage towards any other person all things considered. Kids who discover that being vicious is cool from their kin might happen to brutal ways of life that land them in jail or more awful. All things considered, tackle your concern serenely and by working it out. In the event that somebody attempts to drive you into a battle, be the greater individual and leave.

Young men who witness their folks being savage are two times as prone to be brutal themselves, so what might do in the event that they see a sibling that they truly gaze upward to being fierce?

- **ACT NATURALLY**

Help your kin to regard themselves by continuously acting naturally. Do this by acting naturally. Seek after the things that you love and don't allow prominent sentiment to influence you. Be individual and fail to remember the patterns and doing what will make you the most famous. By doing these things, your kin will figure out how to be certain about their own. Discuss more with your kin so you become truly close, it helps assemble your trust.

➢ SAFEGUARD OTHERS

Show your kin that they ought to constantly stand up for the little man and safeguard individuals who merit insurance by doing likewise yourself. No one can really tell, that young child getting beat up at school might not have a sibling that is ready to safeguard him. Safeguarding the vulnerable will show your kin how to be great individuals and will make them regard you significantly more.

➢ MAKE THE WISEST DECISION

Make the best decision, particularly when it's hard. This likewise implies saying 'sorry' or conceding when you've accomplished something wrong. You maintain that your kin should have the option to do likewise, to continuously make the best choice. This will make both of you better individuals.

FOSTERING A DECENT RELATIONSHIP

- **INVEST ENERGY WITH YOUR KIN**

The most ideal way to begin having a superior relationship with your kin is to invest energy with them. Hang out, play, end up in a good place... it doesn't make any difference. Do anything feels appropriate for you. This will give you extraordinary recollections together and furthermore construct a kinship past the kin relationship.

- **CONSTRUCT THEIR SELF-ASSURANCE**

You believe that your kin should have extraordinary self-assurance, so assist them with helping their certainty. Praise them when they merit it, assist them with building abilities and get more intelligent, and assist them with doing things that they can be glad for. This will likewise satisfy you on the grounds that not exclusively will they be pleased with themselves however you'll be glad for them as well.

➢ CONSTRUCT AND KEEP THEIR TRUST

If you have any desire to have a decent connection with your kin, you ought to have a ton of trust between you. At the point when they let you know something, don't proceed to tell your folks. Keep things just among you, except if your kin requests that you tell your folks. In the event that you can't confide in one another, you'll likely have a hard relationship until the end of your lives.

You ought to likewise fabricate their trust by making a protected spot for them to come and discuss their concerns. You ought to never chuckle at them or judge them for the things they tell you, so they realize they can constantly come to you unafraid of how you'll respond.

➢ ALLOW THEM TO ACT NATURALLY

Try not to attempt to make them into you and don't be furious on the off chance that they don't necessarily pursue the choices you wish they would. Regard that they are their own people and celebrate them, simply how they are. Attempt to do a portion of their exceptional side interests with them or if nothing else talk with and get some information about it every once in a while.

➢ SEE THINGS ACCORDING TO THEIR POINT OF VIEW

You will likely differ about stuff here and there. That is exactly how being kin goes. Yet when you contend or when they accomplish something you can't help contradicting, attempt to see things according to their perspective. Feel for them and comprehend that they're presumably making an honest effort. This will assist with eliminating battles.

- **SEEING THINGS ACCORDING TO THEIR VIEWPOINT SHOULD LIKEWISE BE POSSIBLE CONSISTENTLY.**

Valuing their battles throughout everyday life and regarding them for what they go through will give you both a superior regard for the other.

➢ ASSIST THEM WITH THEIR CONCERNS

At the point when they have issues, help them! Try not to do what needs to be done for them yet tell them the best way to fix it themselves. This will improve their life over the long haul yet it will likewise foster the kinship between you.

Notwithstanding, assuming they decline your assistance, you want to regard their desires. Everything you can manage is to show up for them in the event that they come up short or need assistance still.

➢ ENERGIZE YOUR KIN

Urge your kin to go out and do what they need with their lives. Urge them to try the impossible. Urge them to be better individuals. These things will assist them with accomplishing more throughout everyday life and to be more joyful individuals. This will save you from the disaster of seeing them hurt and languishing.

➢ PAY SPECIAL ATTENTION TO YOUR KIN

Your kin could sometime run into inconvenience, whether they're getting harassed or they're spending time with some unacceptable group.

Regardless of the circumstance, you ought to stand up for and safeguard your kin, assisting them with pursuing better decisions as needs be. You may not necessarily win these fights, yet your kin won't ever need to uncertainty the amount you love them and you won't ever need to feel remorseful about not doing what's necessary to safeguard them.

EXCEEDING ALL EXPECTATIONS

- **SOLACE YOUR KIN WHEN THEY'RE MISERABLE**

A decent embrace and a caring word will go far when your kin is miserable. Allow them to discuss their concerns (or not discuss their concerns!) and simply show them that you're there for them by giving them an embrace until they feel significantly improved.

- **DO DECENT THINGS FOR YOUR KIN**

You can do decent things for them by doing what they request that you do occasionally, or by doing arbitrarily pleasant things for them, such as making them breakfast or assisting them with tidying up their room.

- **HELP THEN HAVE A POSITIVE OUTLOOK ON THEMSELVES**

Offer your kin praises when they accomplish something cool or great. Let them know that they look decent every once in a while or praise their garments. This can cause them to feel quite a bit better about themselves.

➢ GET THEM SMART GIFTS

At the point when occasions or birthday events roll around, get them presents that are great for them, not simply something truly nonexclusive that anybody would get. Contemplate what helps you to remember them or things that you've done together. Ponder things they've said they preferred or that they needed. Ponder the things that they'd require. This will assist you with getting the ideal gift.

➢ BE LIBERAL

Share what you have with your kin. If they have any desire to acquire your stuff, let them. Assuming that you get some sweets, share it with them. Never do things like this anticipating something consequently. Do it since you need to be a decent sibling.

➢ VISIT AND CALL THEM

Assuming your kin is voyaging or lives elsewhere, or when you are more established and have moved far separated, call them or visit them when you can to show them that you ponder them. Try not to allow your relationship to separate as a result of the distance however rather create it a solid association that can cross any distance.

CHAPTER TWO

WAYS OF DRAWING NEAR TO YOUR SIBLING

It is enjoyable to grow up with a sibling, particularly in the event that you are near one another. However much it is cute having a sister or sisters around, siblings make growing up more invigorating with their energy and active spirits.

Nonetheless, a few people have siblings yet didn't have the chance to have a cozy relationship with them. It may be the case that they experienced childhood in various conditions, like on account of broken families, or an enormous age hole.

Could it be past the point of no return for kin in this present circumstance to have a more grounded bond?

The response is 'no.' The length of these people are as yet alive, there will constantly be an opportunity to work on the relationship.

➢ TRY NOT TO BE EXCESSIVELY SEVERE.

It is a typical issue with oldest or more seasoned kin. They will generally be severe, even with the end result of being cruel, towards their more youthful family. In the event that you are the most established, try not to be excessively firm with your kin.

Attempt to be more permissive towards your sibling to try not to scare him. Grin and snicker with him. Give him the freedom to choose for him and abstain from limiting him from leaving the house, spending time with his companions, and doing what he enjoys.

You can offer him guidance and updates about the outcomes of wrong choices.

- **MESS AROUND HIM.**

In association with no. 1, permit yourself to get or trade messes with your sibling. Try not to fly off the handle at whatever point he prods you since that forms the wall between you. You can toss your jokes at him, yet ensure that you don't get uncaring.

- **BE AVAILABLE TO HIM ABOUT YOUR VIEWPOINTS OR ISSUES.**

In the event that you maintain that your sibling should be available to you, begin by being straightforward with him. When he feels that you trust him, he is bound to believe you back. Eventually, he will be more happy with opening dependent upon you too.

- **GUARANTEE HIM THAT HE CAN CONVERSE WITH YOU ABOUT ANYTHING.**

Likewise, letting him know that you are continuously able to tune in and support him will assist your sibling with being more happy with opening up. It is critical in overcoming any barrier between you. Obviously, you shouldn't compel him to open dependent upon you since that would be awkward for him. Simply sit tight for him to be prepared to completely trust you.

- **SPEND TIME WITH HIM AND HIS COMPANIONS.**

One more method for being close with your sibling is by getting to realize his companions better. You can advise your sibling to welcome his companions over for a grill party or inquire as to whether they might want to go along with you on an away excursion. When you become companions with his companions, he will understand that you are not a 'downer', so he would be more open to holding with you. You can likewise present your sibling and his companions to your own arrangement of companions.

➢ BOND WITH HIM AT HOME.

Other than holding with him outside with his companions, you can likewise spend time with your sibling at home. You can watch motion pictures or your #1 television series together while devouring popcorn, French fries, pizza, and your other most loved food varieties. Obviously, you can remember your different kin or guardians for your holding meeting.

- **ASSIST HIM WITH HIS ERRANDS, SCHOOL WORKS, OR WORK STUFF.**

The most effective way to win your sibling's finished trust is by assisting him with achieving his undertakings, particularly at whatever point he is packing and excessively pushed. Assuming he is excessively occupied with his work or studies, and you realize he lacks the capacity to deal with different things, you can step in. For example, you can propose to do his clothing or tidy up his room.

You may likewise propose to assist him with school tasks, schoolwork, or business related exercises.

- **GIVE HIM PRESENTS, EVEN WITH PRACTICALLY NO UNIQUE EVENT.**

Giving presents to your relatives on Christmas or their birthday events is a typical motion. In any case, on the off chance that you would do it even with next to no event, that sounds more paramount, truly. Your sibling will unquestionably see the value in even little presents from you, like a cap, mug, or shirt. Your mindfulness would make him at more simplicity with you around.

➢ HUMOR HIM WITH FOOD.

By and large, both young men and young ladies can't avoid food. Subsequently, to draw nearer to your sibling, then, at that point, enjoy food. You can welcome him for snacks at McDonald's or have pizzas conveyed at home at whatever point you are marathon watching together, or he is occupied with the everyday schedule stuff.

➢ VISIT HIM AT WHATEVER POINT YOU CAN.

On the off chance that you are not living under a similar rooftop, being nearer to him is as yet conceivable. If conceivable, you can visit him consistently, as one time each week, and carry a food to him. That would cause him to feel more focused on, particularly assuming he is just away for studies. Keeping an eye on him generally would be sweet.

- **WELCOME HIM OVER OCCASIONALLY.**

Or then again you can do it the reverse way around. Beside visiting him, you can likewise welcome him to see you. Then, at that point, at whatever point he comes, you can get him a decent eatery and go out on the town to shop together. On the off chance that you have your own family as of now, you can allow him to remain with you for some time so he can bond with your companion and children.

- **BE CLOSE WITH HIS SWEETHEART OR SPOUSE.**

Being strong of his adoration life would be a big deal to your sibling. He would doubtlessly be happy when he sees that you are obliging his significant other or sweetheart well. Beside holding with them both, you can spend time with his accomplice alone. You need to cherish her as your own sister also.

- **SAY 'SORRY' AT WHATEVER POINT YOU AFFRONT HIM.**

It is normal for kin to quibble at times. In any case, over-familiarity can obliterate any relationship, including that of kin. Thus, be aware of your words and treatment toward your sibling. At the point when you realize you have insulted him, be sufficiently modest to apologize to him.

- **REQUEST THAT HE BE YOUR CHAPERONE.**

At whatever point you have a date and are not happy going alone, why not request that your sibling go with you? It won't just assist you with having a solid sense of safety with your date, however it can likewise reinforce the connection between you as you get to know each other.

- **GET HIM A TICKET FOR HIS NUMBER ONE BAND'S SHOW.**

Is your sibling a music darling? If indeed, figure out who his number one specialists are. Then, at that point, when you find that one of them would have a show close by, furtively purchase a ticket/tickets for it. Shock your sibling with it, and he would unquestionably cherish you even more.

➢ GO ON AN UNDERTAKING WITH HIM.

16. On the off chance that your sibling is a friendly or dynamic individual, experience will certainly be energizing to him. Welcome him to drawing in exercises like climbing, setting up camp, swimming, and other fun proactive tasks. He would definitely be more appreciative for having an in a hurry sister or sibling like you.

CHAPTER THREE

CHARACTERISTICS OF A DECENT SIBLING

Everybody loves to have adoring kin who can go about as their closest companions as well. Kin are not simply associated by blood. Their season of growing up together has established their strong bond.

Nonetheless, kin are noticeably flawed as well. Regardless of whether a similar blood runs in their veins, they actually have various characters and viewpoints. Hence, they can't keep away from mistaken assumptions some of the time.

- **STRONG OF THEIR KIN**

A decent kin upholds their family to their greatest advantage and dreams. They are among their top team promoters and would support them uproariously among the group. Also, they are glad for their kin's accomplishments, so they celebrate with them. They likewise assist them with achieving their objectives.

➢ MINDFUL AUDIENCE

Very much like an old buddy, a tremendous sibling or sister will continuously be accessible to pay attention to their kin. They can pay attention to their tirades, heartbreaks, and invigorating stories without judgment. They will actually want to sit with them until the hours shortly after midnight just to stand by listening to their kin discuss their pulverizes or separations.

➢ EVER SMART

A decent sister or sibling doesn't fail to remember their kin's birthday events. On Christmas and other exceptional events, you can expect superb presents and impromptu get-together from them. Additionally, they will energetically go to their graduations, school exhibitions, and other extraordinary occasions.

➢ CAN BE RELIED UPON

Great kin are dependable. At the point when their sister or sibling imparts confidential to them, they will keep that inside them. They are probably not going to deceive their kin in any event, during their misconceptions.

➢ PLAIN AND FAIR WITH THEM

One more quality of a decent kin is being forthright and fair with their siblings. At the point when they realize their kin need to hear reality, they will tell it straight. For that reason they are great at reproaching.

➢ AMENDS THEIR ERRORS

In association with no. 7, a decent kin reprimands and rectifies their family when required. They don't endure bad behaviors.

➢ OFFERS GUIDANCE FROM THEIR OWN INSIGHT

Particularly the more established ones, kin who care about their family will offer them useful and supportive guidance. More often than not, they will involve their own encounters as their wellspring of shrewdness.

➢ SHOWS REGARD FOR THEIR FOLKS

Great kin are great impacts on one another. Quite possibly of the best impact an incredible sister or sibling can have on their different kin is regarding their folks. They will train them to continue regarding and complying with them regardless of whether their folks are flawed.

➢ GREAT PIONEER

A decent more seasoned kin can be a magnificent pioneer to the more youthful ones in the family. They are great at navigation and can be firm in executing house rules. In addition, they model how to be a decent youngster to their folks by stepping up to the plate and do family errands. Obviously, they are additionally great at assigning errands.

➢ DOESN'T CONTEND WITH KIN

You can likewise say that a kin is great in the event that they don't consider their family to be rivals. They are not envious of them. As far as they might be concerned, the progress of their kin is their prosperity as well. Some are in any event, able to forfeit their own fantasies just to help their kin.

➢ STARTS COMPROMISE

Besides, during a misconception, the full grown kin won't just apologize for their errors. They can likewise save their pride and start compromise. Beside not having any desire to disturb their folks, they simply love their kin enough not to allow a day to pass by with sorrows between them.

- **EXCUSES AND DOESN'T HOLD HARD FEELINGS**

An extraordinary sibling or sister has a decent heart that doesn't stay out of resentment and contempt. They can excuse their kin and let go of their resentment and feelings of despair as a result of them.

- **GIVES TIME TO BOND WITH THEIR KIN**

In spite of running their own lives and being occupied with their vocation, a magnificent kin will continuously carve out opportunity to find their family. They additionally start family get-together and orchestrate dates and occasion trips.

- **DEALS WITH THEM**

You don't need to ask a superb kin to deal with a debilitated sister or sibling. As somebody who genuinely cherishes their family, they will actually want to forfeit anything they are doing to really focus on a kin out of luck.

➢ PATIENT AND UNDERSTANDING

A decent kin has long tolerance and wide comprehension towards their family. In spite of the fact that false impressions and contentions can't be kept away from in some cases, they will in any case make an honest effort to tolerate the imperfections of their kin.

➢ GOOD EXAMPLE

Obviously, a capable kin fills in as a genuine guide to their family. This is principally valid for the oldest kin. They will give their all to be capable children, particularly as understudies. They will concentrate on their examples consistently and endeavor to have high grades. Some even saved getting an adoration life while they are still in school to keep away from interruptions.

➢ APPEALS TO GOD FOR THEIR KIN

One more quality of a decent kin is being devoted. Their adoration for their family causes them to argue to God for their security, great wellbeing, direction, and achievement. They comprehend that they can't generally be together, yet God will continuously accompany them. Thus, they request that the Master hold them under His assurance generally.

HOW MIGHT I IMPROVE AS A SIBLING?

Acknowledge your kin how they are and attempt give them trust in their reality. The foundation of each and every relationship is acknowledgment and wellbeing.

Converse with them, pose inquiries about their temperament, issues, accomplishments this will help in creating trust among you and your kin.

Support them when they are going through terrible times.

Educate them concerning your mix-ups and how they ought to keep away from these errors that you have made in your life.

Help them in tracking down their objectives in expert and individual life.

Safeguard them actually as well as intellectually and mental by showing them encounters of life.

Attempt to assist them with their undertaking without making them reliable on you.

Regard their security and give them space.

Try not to meddle in there choice, however attempt to give helpful ideas.

CHAPTER FOUR

CONCLUSION

We as a whole need great kin, particularly during difficult situations. The world will be a superior spot in the event that each individual will be a decent sibling or sister to everybody. There will be no covetousness, pride, envy, and scorn. All things being equal, there might be genuine love.

Why not make it your objective to be a superior sibling or sister to your kin? Appreciate each experience that you are still attached. Sometime in the future, when you have your own lives and families, you would unquestionably miss being with one another.

Thusly, begin to be a decent kin to them now. It will likewise do right by your folks and blissful. Sometime in the future, when you have become old, you would love esteeming and taking great consideration of your family, including your kin.

www.ingramcontent.com/pod-product-compliance
Lightning Source LLC
LaVergne TN
LVHW050346160826
845677LV00014B/3812

* 9 7 9 8 8 4 8 7 0 5 1 7 1 *